AMERICAN DEBATES AND SPEECHES

EXAMINING "AIN'T I A WOMAN?" BY SOJOURNER TRUTH

Alex David

Enslow PUBLISHING

Published in 2021 by Enslow Publishing, LLC
101 W. 23rd Street, Suite 240, New York, NY 10011

Library of Congress Cataloging-in-Publication Data

Names: David, Alex, author.
Title: Examining "Ain't I a Woman?" by Sojourner Truth / Alex David.
Description: New York : Enslow Publishing, 2021. | Series: American debates and speeches | Includes bibliographical references and index. | Audience: Grades 6-12.
Identifiers: LCCN 2019012593| ISBN 9781978515048 (library bound) | ISBN 9781978515031 (pbk.)
Subjects: LCSH: Truth, Sojourner, 1799-1883. | African American abolitionists—Biography. | African American women—Biography. | Abolitionists—United States—Biography. | Social reformers—United States—Biography.
Classification: LCC E185.97.T8 D38 2020 | DDC 326/.8092 [B] —dc23
LC record available at https://lccn.loc.gov/2019012593

Printed in the United States of America

To Our Readers: We have done our best to make sure all websites in this book were active and appropriate when we went to press. However, the author and the publisher have no control over and assume no liability for the material available on those websites or on any websites they may link to. Any comments or suggestions can be sent by email to customerservice@enslow.com.

Portions of this book originally appeared in *Sojourner Truth's "Ain't I a Woman?"* by Corona Brezina.

Photos Credits: Photo research by Bruce Donnola
Cover Bettmann/Getty Images; pp. 5, 6, 19, 41, 52 MPI/Archive Photos/Getty Images; p. 7 Marka/Alamy Stock Photo; pp. 9, 22 Universal History Archive/Universal Images Group/Getty Images; p. 11 GraphicaArtis/Archive Photos/Getty Images; p. 15 Everett Collection Inc/Alamy Stock Photo; p. 16 Corbis Historical/Getty Images; p. 24 The Miriam and Ira D. Wallach Division of Art, Prints and Photographs: Print Collection, The New York Public Library. "Prophet Matthias" The New York Public Library Digital Collections. 1835 - 1899. http:/digitalcollections.nypl.org/items/5e66b3e9-1f4a-d471-e040-e00a180654d7; p. 26 Newberry Library, Chicago, Illinois, USA/Bridgeman Images; p. 29 Interim Archives/Archive Photos/Getty Images; p. 30 Ohio Historical Society, Columbus, OH/Library of Congress; p. 33 Jeff Greenberg/Universal Images Group/Getty Images; p. 38 Kean Collection/Archive Photos/Getty Images; p. 44 Patti McConville/Alamy Stock Photo; p. 53 Jim West/Alamy Stock Photo; Ozz Design/Shutterstock.com (back cover and interior pages background pattern); pashabo/Shutterstock.com (interior pages American flag patterns); Midwaves/Shutterstock.com, Leonid Zarubin/Shutterstock.com (interior pages abstract textures and patterns)

CONTENTS

INTRODUCTION

In 1843, Sojourner Truth met a Quaker woman as she was walking along a sandy road in Long Island. The woman questioned Truth's name, "Where does thee get a name such as that?" Sojourner Truth explained that after being freed from slavery, she had asked God for a new name. Sojourner Truth said, "Thy name is Truth and Truth shall be my abiding name till I die."

At birth, Sojourner was given the first name Isabella. After she was freed from slavery, Sojourner Truth unclasped the constraints of her old name and renamed herself: Sojourner Truth.

This strong name fit the exceedingly charismatic orator. Truth's speeches shook people. Her voice was often described as booming and thunderous. Eliza Leggett, a friend of Truth's, wrote, "her presence was so powerful, her magnetism, so great, her personal appearance so majestic."

Sojourner Truth was an antislavery, women's rights speaker. She traveled around America giving speeches to audiences. Often invited to homes, children sat on her lap, adults gave her the head of the table. People wanted to hear her exceptional ideas. She was funny and smart, often making sarcastic comments to her audience. She drew people in. It was the 1851 Women's Rights Convention that made her "Ain't I a Woman?" speech legendary.

It was a spring day—May 29, 1851. Sojourner Truth may have felt unwelcome at the event. She had just taken a boat on Lake Erie from Buffalo to Ohio. She arrived in Cincinnati after having, as she said in a letter to Amy Post, "a beautiful passage" up the lake. However, at the hotel where people from the convention were staying, she was the only person of color and was avoided by Frances Dana Gage and Hannah Tracy Cutler, the two white women who were in charge of the convention. Sojourner Truth carried the book she had written and was now selling: *Narrative of Sojourner Truth*. Surprised by her presence, a man, Lucius Hine, cheekily joked to Gage and Cutler that Truth must be one of the delegates to their convention. Sojourner Truth was unfamiliar to Gage and Cutler, yet she had the powerful presence of a queen. Cutler later recognized their bad behavior, "I fear we did not feel ready to give her as royal a welcome as her merits deserved."

This is a photograph of Sojourner Truth from around 1870.

The convention itself was held in a church. It was probably quite chilly. Speakers' voices echoed through the rafters. Truth sat in the front. The convention was meant to encourage women's rights and equality, and Truth's presence shone

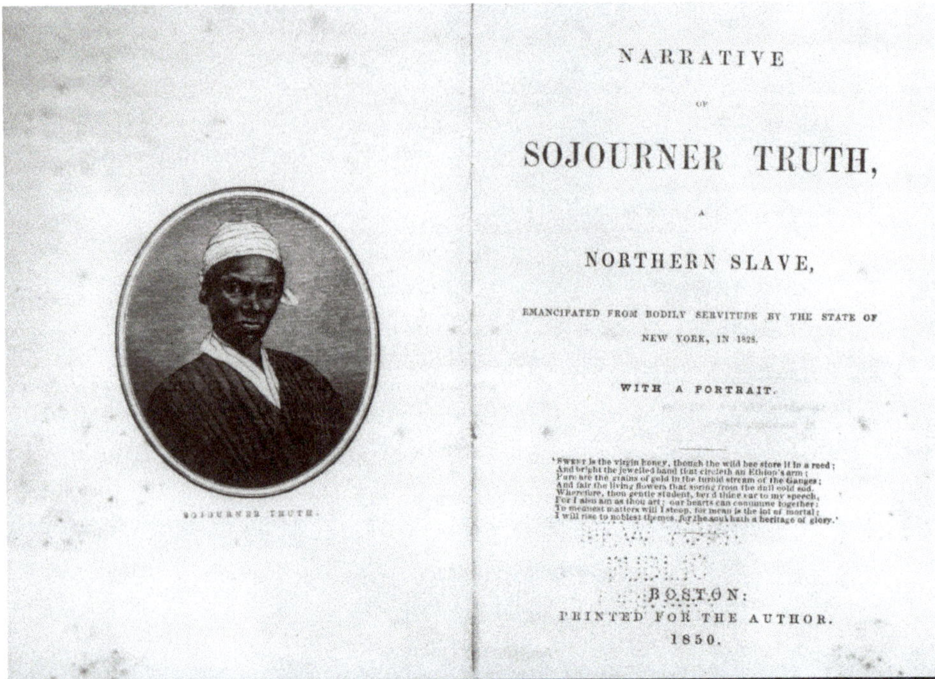

SOJOURNER TRUTH.

NARRATIVE

OF

SOJOURNER TRUTH,

A

NORTHERN SLAVE,

EMANCIPATED FROM BODILY SERVITUDE BY THE STATE OF NEW YORK, IN 1828.

WITH A PORTRAIT.

'SWEET is the virgin honey, though the wild bee store it in a reed;
And bright the jewelled band that circleth an Ethiop's arm;
Pure are the grains of gold in the turbid stream of the Ganges;
And fair the living flowers that spring from the dull cold sod.
Wherefore, thou gentle student, bend thine ear to my speech,
For I also am as thou art; our hearts can commune together:
To meanest matters will I stoop, for mean is the lot of mortal;
I will rise to noblest themes, for the soul hath a heritage of glory.'

BOSTON:
PRINTED FOR THE AUTHOR.
1850.

Sojourner Truth published her book, *Narrative of Sojourner Truth*, in 1850.

light on a major complication of this time: the intersection of equality for women and equality for African Americans. Some white women, like Jane Swisshelm, the editor of the *Pittsburgh Saturday Visiter* only wanted to progress equality for white women. Swisshelm wanted women to be able to own property, but she didn't support women's right to vote. Furthermore, at the conference, she did not want rights for women to be intermixed with "the rights of color."

Sojourner Truth's "Ain't I a Woman?" speech is often imagined as a captivating speech where Truth states, "Ain't I a Woman?" at the end of each line. However, there are many different versions of the speech as different people recorded it. Sojourner Truth could not read or write. The speech may not have been remembered correctly. It is possible that Sojourner Truth may not have made a complete speech at all, but rather courageously interjected remarks refuting what the speakers at the convention were saying. She may have actually said, "Aren't I a woman?" once or possibly, even more assertively, "I am a woman!"

Frances Dana Gage was one of the people who recorded her words, years later. She did so with the soft fabrication that comes from memory. However, Gage did successfully record the feeling of triumph that was so present that day. Truth moved people when she spoke. She could quiet an audience into thoughtful silence or raise them up into applause. This speech marks an important milestone in Sojourner Truth's life and in the abolition and women's suffrage movement.

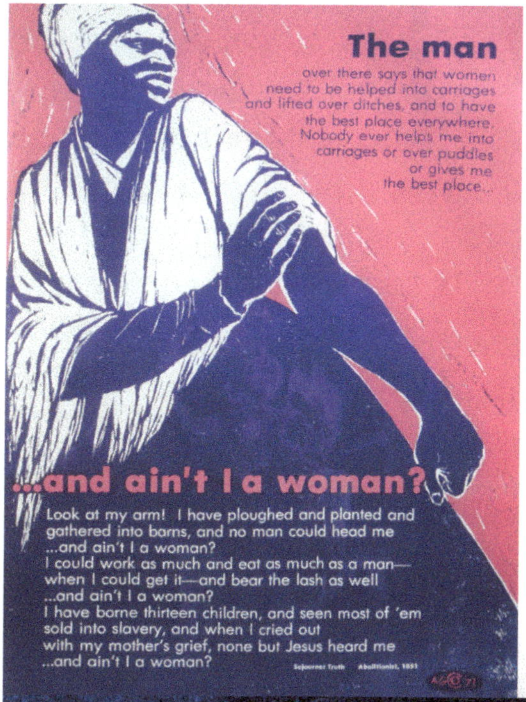

Sections of Truth's speech, as recorded by Frances Dana Gage, are shown here.

CHAPTER ONE

THE NEED FOR CHANGE

In 1797, Isabella was born to her mother, Elizabeth, and her father, James. She was born on a farm run by a Dutch owner. Isabella's parents are sometimes referred to as Mau-Mau Bett and Bomefree. Both had African heritage. Isabella's grandparents had made the middle passage, that horrible trip from Africa to America on slave ships. History sometimes confuses Sojourner Truth as being African. However, she was not. She was of African descent but born in America. Both of Isabella's parents were slaves. She too was a slave.

Slavery in Early America

Slavery took root in the American colonies during the first half of the seventeenth century. It developed differently in the Northern and Southern colonies. Agriculture sustained the Southern economy, and agriculture depended on slave labor. Slaves worked on huge plantations, tending commercial crops such as cotton, tobacco, rice, and sugarcane. Small

Enslaved people had to do different kinds of labor. Here is an illustration of slaves performing agricultural work in Virginia.

landowners often owned only a few slaves; the owners of large plantations could own hundreds.

The Northern economy was far less dependent on slave labor. Slaves in the North worked on small farms, in private homes, or in small businesses or industries. Although slaves made up a large portion of the population in some areas, Northern slaves were more likely to be isolated from other black people. Many Northern slaveholders owned only one or two slaves.

During the American Revolution (1775–1783), patriotic Americans championed the cause of liberty. Many people believed that the ideals in the Declaration of Independence conflicted with the realities of slavery. Some slaveholders, including George Washington, freed their slaves or granted them freedom in their wills. After the revolution, Northern states began taking measures to restrict or eliminate slavery. Vermont became the first state in the country to ban slavery in 1777.

The framers of the U.S. Constitution compromised on the issue of slavery. They did so because Southern slaveholders threatened to withdraw from the Union if the institution was threatened. The Constitution stated that a slave counted as "three-fifths" of a person in population statistics. It authorized the enactment of fugitive slave laws so that owners could reclaim escaped slaves. A clause allowed the foreign slave trade to continue for twenty years after the drafting of the Constitution. Congress outlawed the foreign slave trade in 1808.

[illegible]orge Washington is shown here at age sixty [illegible] in his [illegible] 1799, he freed his slaves. He was the only one of the Founding Fathers who owned slaves to free them.

By the time Truth was born, every Northern state except New York and New Jersey had eliminated slavery. And, in fact, New York, where Isabella lived, had the largest population of enslaved people. In 1799, the New York legislature decreed that all slaves born after July 4, 1799, would eventually be freed—women would gain their freedom at age twenty-five and men at twenty-eight. An 1817 law established that slaves born before 1799 would be freed on July 4, 1827.

Even as the North gradually abolished slavery, the practice became more deeply entrenched in the South. Slave owners argued that slavery was necessary for the health of the economy. They increasingly claimed that it benefited both masters and slaves. By the mid-nineteenth century, Southern slaveholders generally rejected the idea in the Declaration of Independence that "all men are created equal." Southern leaders such as John C. Calhoun claimed that slaves, being of African descent, were naturally inferior to whites. According to Calhoun, the slave system created a stable foundation for society. He also argued that slaves would be worse off if they were freed.

Antislavery Americans

A major point of contention between the North and the South was the prospect of allowing slavery in the western territories. Northerners, especially those in the Free-Soil movement, wanted to reserve the territories for independent settlers in search of new opportunities. Southerners believed that the slave system should be allowed to expand. They felt that if slavery was banned in the West, antislavery

Death or Liberty

There was a lot of fear surrounding freed people and enslaved people who had escaped. Many Southern slaveholders worried that these people would cause an uprising. They were desperately worried that the plantation system would be destroyed.

In 1800, there was one such revolt. An enslaved person named Gabriel Prosser recruited more than a thousand armed slaves with the intention of capturing Richmond, Virginia, and asking the governor to free him and the other slaves. Prosser had learned to read and had many artisanal skills. He subscribed to many of the ideas of the American Revolution and he planned to carry a flag that said "Death or Liberty." However, the weather prevented the army from crossing a bridge. Prosser escaped on a boat and was turned into the police by another slave. Later, he was hanged for his rebellion to be free.

advocates might try to completely abolish slavery. A series of compromises kept the United States from falling apart over the issue. Yet neither side felt that the matter had been satisfactorily resolved.

The abolitionist movement in the North began with religious revivals and antislavery sentiments within religious groups such as the Quakers. In 1831, an abolitionist named William Lloyd Garrison founded the abolitionist newspaper, *The Liberator*. He helped establish the American Antislavery Society in 1833. By the 1840s, abolitionists had organized the Underground Railroad, an antislavery network that helped escaped slaves on their journey toward freedom. Although a relatively small percentage of Americans took an active part in the abolitionist movement, abolitionists made their cause a national issue.

The South reacted defensively to abolitionist efforts. Southern slave owners refused to acknowledge the abolitionists' appeals and often banned antislavery publications. Some Southerners believed that the movement was a Northern plot for social, political, and economic dominance. They claimed that abolishing slavery would destroy the agricultural way of life in the South. Even before the abolitionist movement gained a foothold in the North, political extremists in the South threatened to secede from the Union if they felt that their lifestyle and livelihoods were in peril.

Tensions between the North and South increased after the 1850 Fugitive Slave Act was passed. The measure allowed Southern slaveholders to track down and seize runaway slaves, even when the slaves had escaped to the

North. The rift between the two sides widened throughout the 1850s, leading to the secession of eleven Southern states from the Union and eventually the Civil War (1861–1865).

This [illegible] as a stop for the Underground Railroad in New Lyme, Ohio.

Women's Rights

Many white women joined the abolitionist movement as it spread during the 1830s. However, in many meetings, only men were allowed to speak and women were not always permitted to sign resolutions. In 1840, a number of Americans traveled to London for the World Antislavery Convention. Several of the delegates were women, including the famous speaker Lucretia Mott. When they arrived, many British and American men objected to the women speaking or even attending. The women were told to sit behind a curtain in a gallery.

Mott and some other delegates, both male and female, were outraged. Mott met a young woman named Elizabeth Cady Stanton at the convention. They decided to organize a conference that would focus on women's rights. They held the first women's rights convention at Seneca Falls, New York, in 1848. About 300 people, including forty men, arrived on the first day. They discussed controversial issues such

Lucretia Mott was a pacifist. She dedicated her life to working for emancipation and women's rights. She did not believe the Civil War was the right way to free enslaved people.

as property and divorce laws, access to jobs and education, and suffrage, or the right to vote. The organizers had drafted a Declaration of Sentiments based on the Declaration of Independence. The Declaration of Sentiments included a list of twelve resolutions on women's issues, including one that demanded the right to vote. It was signed by approximately 100 people.

Newspapers treated the convention as a joke. Even many abolitionists refused to take women's rights seriously. However, some, like William Lloyd Garrison, supported the cause. But while most men laughed, the women's rights movement spread. Women across the country established women's rights groups. More conventions and meetings followed the historic Seneca Falls Convention.

CHAPTER TWO

FIGHTING TO BE FREE

Isabella called her first owner, "the old Colonel." Colonel Hardenbergh belonged to a wealthy Dutch family of slave-holders that had lived on the land for nearly a century. He owned six or seven slaves, which was more than the typical New York farmer. When Isabella was very young, Colonel Hardenbergh died and his son, Charles, inherited his farm and slaves.

Because Isabella grew up in a Dutch-speaking community, she learned Dutch as her first language. As a child, Isabella was not taught to read or write, as education was forbidden for slaves. However, some enslaved people were invited to church with their owners. It was here, in this early upbringing, that Isabella began to find solace in religion.

Dina Frelinghuysen Hardenbergh, the wife of Colonel Hardenbergh, was heavily involved in religion. She provided the people she owned with an entry point into spirituality by opening the doors to her church.

In 1807 or 1808, Charles Hardenbergh died, and much of his property, including Isabella and her brother, was auctioned off. The Hardenbergh family decided to free James because he was too old to work and was no longer an economic asset.

There were 316 enslaved men, women and children at George Washington's estate, Mount Vernon. They performed jobs in the fields and in the house. Some were blacksmiths or craftsmen.

They also freed Elizabeth so that she could care for him. James and Elizabeth lived in wretched poverty, and both died within a few years.

A storekeeper named John Nealy paid $100 for Isabella and a flock of sheep. His family spoke only English, and they cruelly whipped Isabella when she did not understand orders.

She carried the scars for the rest of her life. Somehow, her father helped arrange for Martin Scriver, a fisherman and innkeeper, to buy her.

Isabella spent her days with the Scrivers gardening, carrying fish, and running errands. They were kinder masters

The Underground Railroad

Created by Quakers, the Underground Railroad was a system designed to subvert slavery. Metaphorically it was treated as a railroad. There were stops and conductors, but in reality it didn't have anything to do with trains. It was a series of safe houses and numerous people, like Harriet Tubman, who helped enslaved people escape slavery. Often hidden by the dark of night, people trying to escape would quietly travel to farmers' barns or houses. They would spend the day hiding in dark, dank places. Maybe the conductors would be able to sneak them some food while they waited until dark to travel to their next stop. Their final destination was usually Canada, although some enslaved people were able to go to Liberia, in Africa. Between 1810 and 1850, about 100,000 people were led to freedom through this intricate network.

than the Nealys were, and Isabella picked up English more quickly. In 1810, the Scrivers sold her to a farmer named John Dumont.

When Isabella was sixteen or seventeen, she fell in love with a slave named Robert, who worked on a neighboring farm. His master forbade him to visit Isabella. One day, when he sneaked away to see her, his owner followed and nearly beat him to death. Dumont intervened, unwilling to have blood spilled on his land. Robert's master led him away and eventually married him to one of his own slaves. Isabella never saw Robert again. Soon afterward, Dumont married her to a fellow slave named Thomas. Isabella had five children between 1815 and 1826.

Under New York law, Isabella would be freed on July 4, 1827. Dumont told her that if she worked extra hard, he would free her a year early. Isabella kept her part of the bargain, even though she had severely injured her hand. When July 4, 1826, arrived, Dumont claimed that her injury had prevented her from putting in enough work and he refused to free her.

A Free and Courageous Woman

Isabella stayed with the Dumonts until late 1826. Late one night, she left with her baby Sophia, believing that God was directing her. She found her way to the Van Wagenens, a nearby antislavery family. When Dumont tracked her down, she told him that she would rather go to jail than return to him. The Van Wagenens paid $25 for the freedom of Isabella and her baby. She worked for the Van Wagenens as a free woman for the next year.

In 1827, Isabella learned that her six-year-old son, Peter, had been sold and taken to Alabama. It was illegal to sell New York slaves to Southern owners. New York was slowly abolishing slavery, but in Alabama, Peter would likely be enslaved for life. Isabella took a course of action that was almost unheard of for a black woman in those days. She filed a complaint

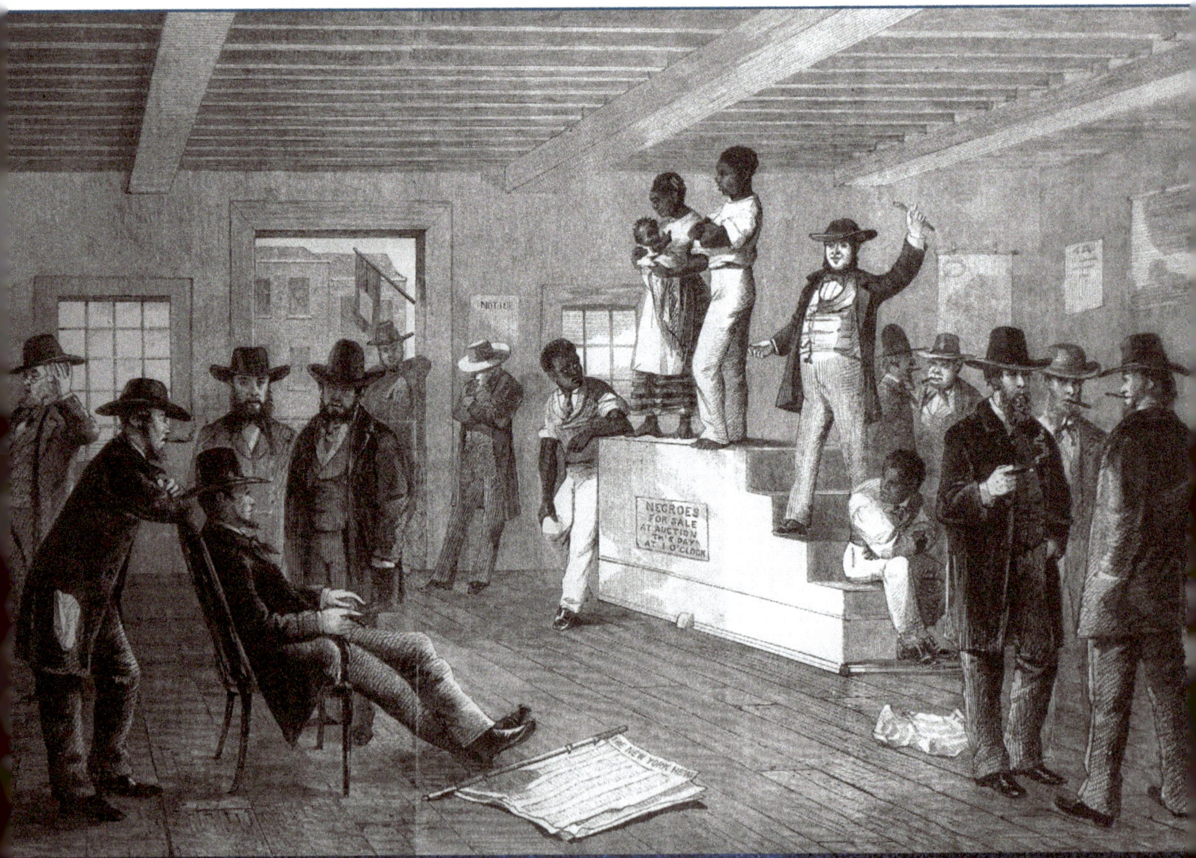

[illegible] depiction of a slave auction in Virginia in [illegible] shows [illegible] brutality of the slave trade. The enslaved family was at risk of being separated and in danger of never seeing one another again.

in court. A jury decided in her favor, and in 1828, Peter was returned to her. His owner had whipped and beaten him until he was covered with scars from head to toe.

A year later, Isabella and Peter left for New York City. Isabella left her other children behind with the Dumonts. In New York City, she worked as a housekeeper in private homes. Isabella also became actively involved in the Methodist Church. She had become a Methodist soon after gaining her freedom. Isabella was a deeply religious person. She threw her whole soul into spreading her faith by preaching, praying, and singing.

Isabella gained a reputation as a stirring preacher. She often spoke at religious meetings. Soon after moving to New York City, she met a religious fanatic named Elijah Pierson while working at a women's shelter. Pierson drew Isabella into a cult led by Robert Matthews. He called his small community Matthias's Kingdom. Isabella gave the group all of her money and did much of the cooking and housework. Matthews treated his followers like servants, though he himself dressed finely and drank from a silver goblet.

In 1834, Pierson died suddenly, and Matthews was accused of poisoning him. Newspapers revealed Matthews as an impostor and publicized some of the cult's bizarre rituals. Though Isabella had not been involved, two members of Matthias's Kingdom made false accusations against her. She sued them for slander and cleared her name in court.

While Isabella was involved in Matthias's Kingdom, her son Peter had been getting into trouble. He could not keep a job and was often caught stealing. His mother thought that an education might give him more opportunities, but he

Sojourner Truth lived under Prophet Matthias, shown here, from [illegible] to 1834. He, like the previous slave owners, often beat her.

skipped school to go dancing. In 1839, Peter signed on as a seaman on a whaling ship. Isabella never saw her son again. They exchanged a few letters up until 1841, but Isabella never learned what happened to Peter after that.

In 1843, Isabella decided to leave New York City. She thought it was a wicked city. Also, she claimed to have been called by God to spread her faith. Isabella quit her job as a domestic. She told her employer that her name was no longer Isabella but Sojourner Truth. Truth planned to travel all over the country, preaching to the people she encountered.

The Second Great Awakening

Truth spent the next few months traveling and speaking at religious meetings. During this time, a religious fervor called the Second Great Awakening was sweeping the country. People attended meetings to pray, listen to speakers, and reaffirm their faith. Truth's preaching and stories often led listeners to laugh and cry. They appreciated her plain speaking and wit. Truth also sang hymns she had written herself.

When winter came, Truth settled down in Northampton, Massachusetts. She joined the Northampton Association, a cooperative community that believed in equality for all people. Many of the members were involved in the abolitionist movement. George Benson, a brother-in-law of the abolitionist William Lloyd Garrison, was one of the leaders. Garrison himself often visited Northampton, as did ex-slave and abolitionist Frederick Douglass.

Douglass wrote his autobiography, *Narrative of the Life of Frederick Douglass, An American Slave*, in 1845. It sold very well, and his success inspired Truth to publish her own autobiography. Because she could not read or write, she dictated her story to a friend named Olive Gilbert. Garrison helped publish *Narrative of Sojourner Truth* in 1850. Truth hoped that she could sell copies of her book when she spoke at meetings. The Northampton Association had closed in 1846, and she

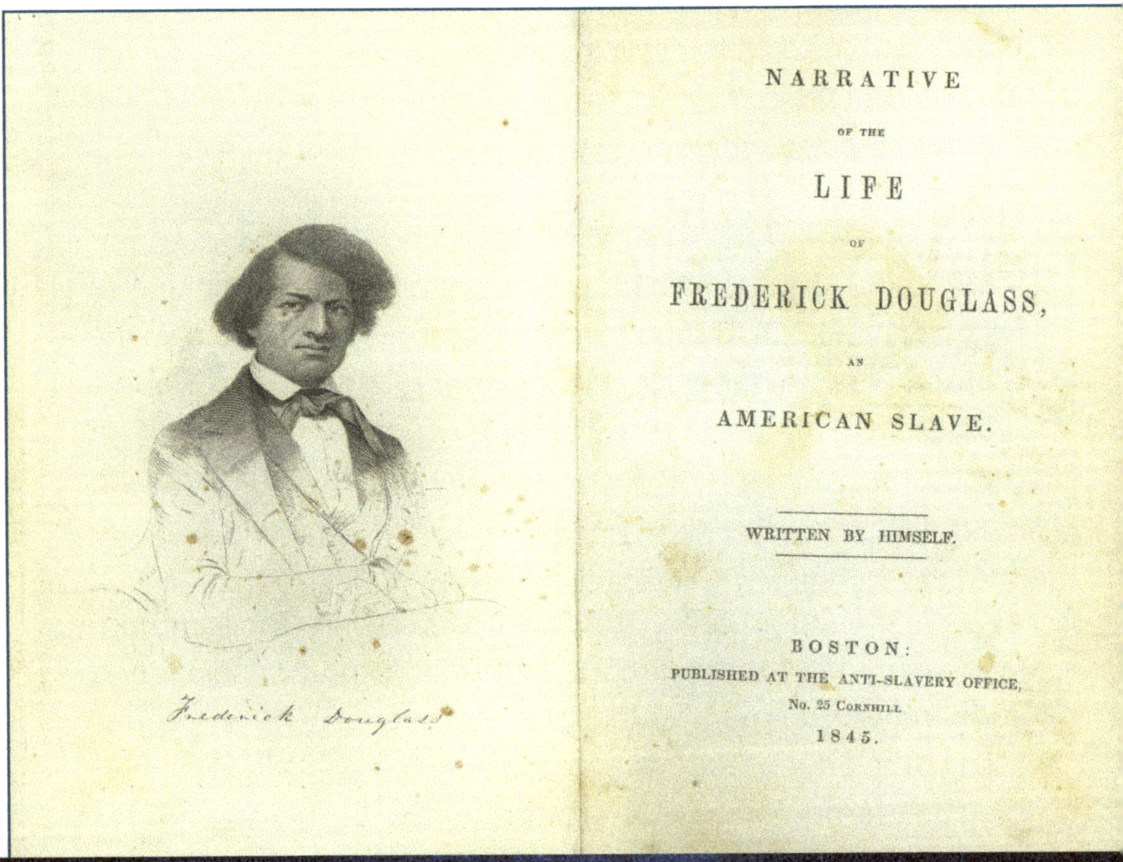

Sojourner Truth hoped to achieve the same success that Frederick Douglass did with his book, *Narrative of the Life of Frederick Douglass*.

had bought a house near Northampton. She needed money to pay the mortgage.

In October 1850, Truth attended a women's rights conference in Worcester, Massachusetts. Many of her old friends from Northampton also attended. Here, Truth made her first documented speech as an activist, arguing for women's rights. In November, she made her first known antislavery speech. Wherever Truth spoke, she offered copies of her book for sale. Truth often had to find creative ways to speak to audiences. If she was rejected from speaking in a church, this did not stop her. She spoke from a tree's stump or the back of a wagon or even a makeshift platform. Often she was heckled by mobs of white people. They smelled of alcohol and physically threatened speakers. One creative solution, Truth found, was to sing gospel songs. This had a calming effect on the listeners and kept her out of harm's way.

After the Worcester convention, Garrison invited Truth to join him and a British abolitionist, George Thompson, on a speaking tour. When Truth arrived in Springfield, Massachusetts, to begin the tour, she found that Garrison had fallen ill. He had stayed at home in Boston to recover. Truth could not afford to go on tour without Garrison's financial help, and she explained the situation to Thompson. He offered to pay her way and treated her as an equal.

In 1851, Truth met Isaac and Amy Post, longtime abolitionists and activists for women's rights. It was the start of a lifelong friendship. Truth stayed with the Posts for much of the winter before heading to Ohio. She planned to attend antislavery meetings and a women's rights conference in Akron.

CHAPTER THREE

"NO UNION WITH SLAVEHOLDERS"

Ohio was a particularly contentious area because of its geographical location. Enslaved people who were trying to reach freedom often used Ohio for stops on the Underground Railroad, as Ohio connected southern states to Canada. If enslaved people could get to Canada, they would be free.

In 1850, the Fugitive Slave Law was passed. President Millard Fillmore called it the "Bloodhound Bill" because of how the law would be used to hunt down ex-slaves and re-enslave them. Black people who were living abroad in Europe were advised to stay there. Many notable black intellectuals became fearful for their lives because of this new law. This is the ominous context that surrounds Sojourner Truth's famous speech. Abolitionists denounced the law. Many traveled through Ohio speaking out against the practice of slavery and the Fugitive Slave Act.

[illegible]outes on the Underground Railroad in Ohio were particularly [illegible] [illegible]quired for getting slaves across to Canada.

Women's Rights and Antislavery

Women as well as men were drawn to the antislavery movement. As they fought for the abolitionist cause, some of the activists also began calling for women's rights. They believed in equality for all people, whether they were white or black, male or female.

ANTI-SLAVERY BUGLE.

"NO UNION WITH SLAVEHOLDERS."

VOL. I. SALEM, O., FRIDAY, SEPTEMBER 5, 1845. NO. 7.

ANTI-SLAVERY BUGLE.
Published every Friday at
Salem, Columbiana Co., O.

JAMES BARNABY, Jr., General Agent.

All remittances to be made, and all letters relating to the pecuniary affairs of the paper, to be addressed (post paid) to the General Agent. Communications intended for insertion to be addressed to the Editors.

Terms:—$1,50 per annum, or $2,00 if not paid within six months of the time of subscribing.

Advertisements making less than a square inserted three times for 75 cents:—one square $1.

Publishing Committee:—Sam'l Brooke, George Garretson, James Barnaby, Jr., David L. Galbreath, Lot Holmes.

BENJAMIN S. JONES,
J. ELIZABETH HITCHCOCK, Editors.

J. H. PAINTER, PRINTER.

From the N. O. Tropic, Extra, of Aug. 14th

IMPORTANT FROM MEXICO.

Arrival of the Water Witch—No Declaration of War—10,000 Mexican Troops on their March to Texas.

We hasten to lay before the readers of the Tropic the latest news from Mexico. The *Water Witch*, Capt. Tennis, left Vera Cruz on the 5th inst. and arrived here between 5 and 6 o'clock this morning.

C. M. CLAY.

From the N. Y. Tribune.

The Lexington Outrage—Opinions in Kentucky.

The Anti-Slavery Bugle was first published in June of 1845. Its motto was, "No Union with Slaveholders."

In the spring of 1851, Truth spent time in Salem, Ohio, an antislavery town. She stayed with Emily and Marius Robinson, who were abolitionists and friends of William Lloyd Garrison. They ran the *Anti-Slavery Bugle*, the only abolitionist paper in the area. The *Bugle* also reported on women's rights issues. In March 1851, it urged all reformers to attend a women's rights convention in Akron.

Frances D. Gage organized the Akron conference. It took place in late May. Truth was the only black person in attendance. A religious group, the Universalists, allowed the conference to meet in its church. Gage was a writer of fiction and poetry, and an ardent supporter of both the abolitionist and women's rights movements. She wrote an account of Truth's Akron address that made the "Ain't I a Woman?" speech a legend. Some historians, however, believe that Gage may have added her own words to the text and changed details of the event to make the story more dramatic.

Frances Gage Poetic Telling of Sojourner Truth's Speech

Sojourner Truth was non-literate. Although friends and listeners recorded many of her speeches, Truth never wrote down her own words. By all reports, she was a moving and charismatic speaker. Today, we will never be able to grasp any more than a shadow of what Truth's audience must have experienced.

Frances Gage wrote her account of Truth's "Ain't I a Woman?" speech in 1863, twelve years after the Akron convention. She published it in the *National Antislavery Standard*, a New York abolitionist newspaper. Truth later included Gage's article in an updated version of *Narrative of Sojourner Truth*.

Gage opens her account with a description of the general hostility of many Americans to the women's rights movement. She uses formal, flowery prose typical of the nineteenth century. Describing Truth's arrival at the church, Gage writes of "seeing a tall, gaunt black woman in a gray dress and white turban, surmounted by an uncouth sun-bonnet, march deliberately into the church, [and] walk with the air of a queen up the aisle." Gage claims that many people were disturbed by a black woman taking part in the conference. She reports that they entreated, "Don't let her speak, Mrs. G. It will ruin us. Every newspaper in the land will have our cause mixed up with abolition." Gage replied merely, "We will see when the time comes."

Truth's Speech

Truth made her speech on the second day of the conference. According to Gage's account, most of the morning had been dominated by men, especially clergymen, arguing the inferiority of women. The audience was unfriendly to the women's rights movement, and the women were afraid to defend their cause. Finally, unasked, Truth stood up and moved to the front of the room. Despite the disapproval of the audience, Gage stood up and announced her: "Sojourner Truth." According to Gage's account, "Every eye was fixed on this almost Amazon form, which stood nearly six feet high, head erect, and eye piercing the upper air like one in a dream . . . She spoke in deep tones, which, though not loud, reached every ear in the house."

[illegible] memorial of Sojourner Truth making her famous speech [illegible] in Battle Creek, Michigan. It is twelve feet high and was created by [illegible] artist, Tina Allen.

Truth opened her speech by pointing out the "racket" over inequality being raised by both antislavery and women's rights advocates. As a black woman, Truth uniquely represented both causes. "Well, chillen," Gage quoted Truth as saying,"Dat man over dar say dat woman needs to be helped into carriages, and lifted over ditches, and to have de best place eberywhar. Nobody eber helps me into carriages, or ober mud-puddles, or gives me any best place . . . And ar'n't I a woman?" In Gage's account, Truth dramatically repeats "Ar'n't I a woman?" four times through her speech. Modern reprints often change it to "Ain't I a woman?"

According to Marius Robinson's version of the speech, Truth goes on to refute the widely held belief that women were weaker than men. "I have plowed and planted and gathered into barns, and no man could head me . . . I could work as much and eat as much as a man—when I could get it—and bear de lash as well." For the listeners in Akron, Truth stood as living proof that women were no less capable than men. Her words also alluded to the evils of slavery and the hardships she had endured.

Truth used a metaphor to attack the idea that women were intellectually inferior to men. "If my cup won't hold but a pint and yourn holds a quart, wouldn't ye be mean not to let me have my little half-measure full?" Truth meant that despite physical differences, such as size, women were not less intelligent than men. Therefore, men should not deny women equal rights on the claim that they were not smart enough to make responsible decisions.

According to Gage, Truth next singled out a minister in the audience. "Den dat little man in black dar, he say woman

Sojourner's Speech Pattern

"It is impossible to transfer it to paper, or convey any adequate idea of the effect it produced upon the audience," wrote Truth's friend Marius Robinson after her "Ain't I a Woman?" speech. He referred in part to her compelling charisma, but he also had a practical difficulty in transcribing Truth's words: her accent.

Many people recorded her speeches in a Southern dialect, thinking that readers would expect a former slave to speak with a Southern accent. But Truth grew up in the North and spoke Dutch as her first language. She probably retained traces of Dutch mannerisms in her speech for her whole life. John Dumont's daughter, Gertrude, claimed that Truth's accent resembled that of the typical uneducated farmer in New York State. According to Frederick Douglass, Truth "cared very little for elegance of speech," but she easily captivated an audience.

can't have as much right as man 'cause Christ wa'n't a woman. Whar did your Christ come from? From God and a woman." She argued that if Eve had truly brought sin to the world, then women should be given the chance to "turn it back and git it right side up again." The audience applauded after each of Truth's points. Summing up the experience, Gage says, "I have never in my life seen anything like the magical influence that subdued the mobbish spirit of the day, and turned the jibes and sneers of an excited crowd into notes of respect and admiration."

Fact Checking of Gage's Account

There is no doubt that Frances D. Gage's account captured the spirit and message of Truth's speech. In her version, Truth calls for equal rights and refers to experiences of her own life. She quotes the Bible, as she did in many other speeches. Although she never learned to read, Truth memorized long passages from the Bible.

Many historians studying Sojourner Truth doubt parts of Gage's account. Most agree on one main point: Gage exaggerated the hostile atmosphere of the Akron women's rights conference. Gage describes a stirring turnaround, but in reality, it is unlikely that Truth truly addressed an unfriendly audience.

The general consensus among historians is that men and women who attended the Akron convention were supportive of the women's rights movement and the abolitionist cause. Some were Truth's close personal friends. The town of Akron welcomed the convention and the local community offered the use of its church for the event. Afterward, twenty-seven newspapers featured accounts of the events, four of them describing Truth's speech. No published report mentions any discord. Some attendees publicly stated that they were delighted with the harmony of the conference and their reception at Akron.

A Kind Audience

Truth faced hostile audiences many times in her life. However, it is likely that she was surrounded by friendly faces at Akron. Women's rights conferences during the nineteenth century generally welcomed black speakers. Frederick Douglass spoke at the historic 1848 Seneca Falls Convention in New York, and Truth attended many other women's rights conferences over the next couple of decades.

It is doubtful that antifeminist men dominated the stage on the day Truth spoke, as Gage claimed. Her friend and host Marius Robinson acted as recording secretary for the conference. He wrote in the *Bugle* that "the business of the convention was principally conducted by women," a statement reiterated in other newspapers. Participants probably debated how far equal rights should extend for women, however, and Truth may have addressed some of their points in her speech.

Other Accounts

In Gage's account, Truth emerged as the star of the conference. Other newspaper articles reported that a number of women spoke powerfully and together made the convention a success. Marius Robinson also wrote a detailed account of Truth's speech. Carleton Mabee, author of a biography of Sojourner Truth, believes that Robinson's report is probably the most authentic record of the speech. Robinson does not mention any hostility. In his account, Truth politely asks, "May I speak a few words?" before beginning. Robinson transcribed Truth's words in proper English rather than the dialect Gage used.

Frances Dana Gage is pictured here around 1840. Gage was from McConnelsville, Ohio. She was an abolitionist and an advocate for women's rights.

Much of his content agrees with Gage's version.

A few historians have questioned the accuracy of Gage's text. She admits, "I have given but a faint sketch of her speech," without mentioning her source. Her version contains one glaring inaccuracy: "I have borne thirteen chillen, and seen 'em mos' all sold off into slavery." Truth had only five children. Some scholars even believe that Gage, not Truth, coined the slogan "Ain't I a woman?" Gage reported that Truth repeated the phrase four times, yet no other account mentions the words "Ain't I a woman?"

Truth is not known to have used the phrase in any other speech, nor did she have a habit of repeating key phrases when she spoke. Gage, however, was a poet and often repeated phrases for emphasis and rhythmic flow. If Truth did use the phrase "Ain't I a woman?" it is likely that Gage, not Sojourner herself, turned it into a recurring refrain throughout the speech.

Newspapers gave a glowing report of the conference and applauded Truth's speech. Truth was also pleased, though she never mentioned the public reaction to her speech. She sent a letter to her friend Amy Post, telling her that she had met many kind friends. "I sold a good many books at the convention and have thus far been greatly prospered." She was slowly paying off her debts, and she soon continued on her speaking tour.

CHAPTER FOUR

AMERICA IN 1850

The 1850s were a turbulent time in America. The country was confused. Were they going to allow slavery to exist or not? What did they value? Profit or people? Today America is a country where people freely disagree with each other and it was no different in the 1850s. Abolitionists refused to back down as southern leaders continued to endorse slavery. Senator Stephen Douglas of Illinois and President Franklin Pierce drafted the Kansas-Nebraska Act in 1854. Its intention was to let new states decide whether or not they should allow slavery. Senator Douglas had intended the act to heal relations between slaveholders and abolitionists, but the gap only widened.

Dred Scott

Feelings intensified when the Supreme Court ruled on the case of *Dred Scott v. John F. A. Sandford*. The Dred Scott decision stated that slaveholders had the right to take their slaves into free states and keep them enslaved. Slaveholders considered the case a major victory, but it spurred the abolitionist movement. In 1859, a white abolitionist named John Brown and several followers seized a federal arsenal at Harpers Ferry in

[illegible] of abolitionists, the Oberlin Rescuers, [illegible] 1859. They are standing outside a jail, where they saved a [illegible] slave named John Price.

present-day West Virginia. Though Brown's effort to start a slave rebellion failed, he alarmed local governments throughout the South.

The presidential election of 1860 forced a final showdown between the two sides. The abolitionist-supported Republican candidate, Abraham Lincoln, defeated three other men to become the sixteenth president of the United States. Within three months of his March 4, 1861, inauguration, eleven states had seceded from the Union and the Civil War was underway.

Battle Creek

In 1857, Truth sold her house in Northampton and bought one in the Spiritualist community of Harmonia, Michigan. She later moved to the nearby town of Battle Creek, where her daughters and grandchildren gathered around her. Though Truth spent much time away traveling, Battle Creek was her home for the rest of her life.

Throughout her years as an activist, Sojourner supported the nonviolent abolition of slavery. In 1861, shortly after the war broke out, a group of pro-Confederacy Democrats tried to arrest her during a speaking tour in Indiana. A new Indiana law forbade blacks from entering the state. A pro-Union military group, called the Home Guard, protected her, and Truth insisted on speaking at a courthouse rally as scheduled. Friends dressed her in red, white, and blue, and advised that she carry a sword or pistol. Truth answered, as written in her autobiography, "I carry no weapon; the Lord will [preserve] me without weapons."

Some abolitionists began to believe during the 1850s that a peaceful solution could never succeed. Although Truth never lost her faith in nonviolence, she proudly supported the Union during the Civil War. One of her grandsons served in the military. Truth went door to door collecting food and clothing for local troops. According to legend, one man refused to give her any donations, and she asked his name. "I am the only son of my mother," he replied. "I am glad there are no more," she shot back, with her characteristic sharp wit.

Sculpting Sojourner Truth

In the late 1850s, writer and abolitionist Harriet Beecher Stowe spent her winters in Rome, Italy. There, she met a sculptor named William Wetmore Story. Stowe recounted some of Truth's stories to the sculptor. Stowe claimed that her descriptions of Truth inspired Story to sculpt a marble statue of an African woman. He called the piece the *Libyan Sibyl* after a mythological figure.

Stowe published an article titled "Sojourner Truth, the Libyan Sibyl" in 1863. Although she admired Truth, Stowe portrays her as naive and a passive stereotype instead of giving an honest description of her vibrant personality. The article describes Truth's 1853 visit to Andover and tells of her early life. Stowe also relates the story of a confrontation with Frederick Douglass at a meeting in Boston. He had become frustrated with the abolitionist movement and was beginning to think that violence could be the only solution. Truth leaped up and cried, "Frederick, is God dead?" Her words shocked the room into silence. The phrase became famous as an affirmation of God's justice.

Stowe's article is filled with inaccuracies, though. Even the famous incident with Douglass did not occur exactly as she describes it. Sojourner later grumbled that she was not from Africa, nor did she ever call anyone "honey," as Stowe claimed. Worst of all, Stowe seemed to think that Sojourner Truth was dead.

[illegible] *Libyan Sibyl* by William Wetmore Story is at the [illegible] Museum of Art. Story carved the statue in 1861. The Libyan Sibyl is a prophetess who predicts the terrible destiny of the African people.

Frances D. Gage published her version of "Ain't I a Woman?" less than a month after "Sojourner Truth, the Libyan Sibyl" appeared. Gage may have wanted to correct Stowe's portrait of Truth as a preacher rather than activist. At one point in her account, however, Gage describes Truth as "quiet and reticent as the 'Libyan statue.'" Stowe's article, however, made Truth a romanticized celebrity, and many Americans now knew her—and sympathized with her—as the Libyan Sibyl.

Emancipation Proclamation

On January 1, 1863, President Lincoln freed all slaves in the Confederacy with his Emancipation Proclamation. In early 1864, Sojourner's friends raised money for her to travel to Washington, DC, and she set out on a tour of the East in the summer. Her beloved fourteen-year-old grandson, Sammy, accompanied her.

When she reached Washington, Truth visited the White House and spoke with Abraham Lincoln. She showed the president her "Book of Life," a scrapbook full of newspaper clippings and autographs of people Truth admired. President Lincoln signed her book, "For Aunty Sojourner Truth, October 29, 1864. A. Lincoln." Later in her life, Truth met presidents Andrew Johnson and Ulysses S. Grant. Truth did not leave Washington until 1868. She had found a new mission when she met the freedmen, or former slaves.

The End of the Civil War

The Civil War ended in 1865. By the end of that year, the Thirteenth Amendment to the Constitution had been ratified.

It outlawed slavery in the United States. Still, freedom offered little security for many freedmen. Most had no money and only meager possessions. Remaining in the South meant enduring so-called black codes, which were laws restricting the rights of blacks to own land and to move about as they pleased. Many began migrating to Northern cities in search of work in the factories, yet even there they faced discrimination.

Freedmen swarmed into Washington even before the war ended. Truth joined the refugee relief effort, working with agencies such as the National Freedmen's Relief Association. She lived in a tidy cottage in a camp called Freedmen's Village and helped teach former slaves new skills. Truth's great hope was that the freedmen would be able to find jobs and cease relying on government aid.

Truth often traveled by streetcar during her time in Washington. Often, the conductors would disregard a black woman signaling the car. On a September day in 1865, a conductor violently tried to push her away, injuring Truth's shoulder. She had him arrested for assault and battery. For the third time in her life, Truth took a case to court and won.

Amendments to the Constitution

The Civil War had changed the nature of activists' causes. Abolitionists had seen their hopes become reality. The Fourteenth Amendment to the Constitution granted black men citizenship, and the Fifteenth Amendment gave them the right to vote. This did not end discrimination against blacks, however, and women of all races were still denied equal rights.

The women's rights movement split into two factions in 1869. The group organized by Elizabeth Cady Stanton and Susan B. Anthony opposed the Fifteenth Amendment if women were not included. The other half of the movement supported the Fifteenth Amendment, believing that black male suffrage was an important step in the fight for equal rights. The groups were also divided on political strategy and a few key issues. Truth urged the two groups to mend their differences, but she continued speaking out for women's rights. Finally, she

Exodus of 1879

The American West promised new opportunities to African Americans who had previously been slaves. The South was a difficult place to find work. Many white Southerners made it difficult for black people to vote or to own land. The West was seen as a land of opportunity and people like Benjamin "Pap" Singleton urged one of the first major African American migrations: an exodus to Kansas.

Between 1877 and 1879, 20,000 freedmen, nicknamed Exodusters, took advantage of the Homestead Act of 1862 and made their homes near the town of Nicodemus. This act provided 160 acres of government land to people who would cultivate the property for at least five years. These newly freed people were citizens of America and the town served as an inspiration to many other communities in the Western prairie.

gave her support to the less radical group that supported the Fifteenth Amendment.

Truth's Plan

Sojourner left Washington discouraged by the plight of the freedmen. Jobs were scarce, and many freedmen lacked food and shelter. Truth proposed that the government reserve parts of the empty western territories for freedmen settlements. She felt that after generations of slavery, freedmen deserved the chance to cultivate their own land rather than live in poverty in the cities.

Truth traveled and spoke out in support of her plan. She even wrote up a petition to present to Congress and collected signatures. In 1871 and 1872, Truth and Sammy toured Kansas, Missouri, and the Midwest promoting resettlement. However, Sojourner could not find support in Washington for her expensive proposal. The government was still reeling from the costs of the Civil War and Reconstruction of the South. Racism also played a role, as these areas were primarily settled by whites at the time.

In 1875, bad news brought Truth back to Battle Creek. Sammy was gravely ill. He died in February, and Truth went into debt to pay for his medical bills and burial. Later in the year, Truth's close friend Frances Titus helped publish a new edition of her autobiography, updating Truth's history and adding part of the "Book of Life." For many years, Titus helped Truth in every way she could and accompanied her on her travels.

To Truth's delight, waves of Southern freedmen decided to relocate to the West in an exodus during the late 1870s. Truth traveled to Kansas with Titus to help with the relief effort on behalf of the refugees. Her dream for the freedmen had come true.

CHAPTER FIVE

THE LEGACY OF SOJOURNER TRUTH

In 1882, Truth was eighty-six years old, suffered from gangrene, and was housebound. She stayed at home in Battle Creek, making her bed each morning, and making her own breakfast each day. She was ill and it was apparent her health wouldn't last much longer. In the early morning hours of November 6, she drifted off into death. The next day, the *Chicago Daily Inter-Ocean* reported that "she was loved by all . . . black and white."

Titus, who had cared for her during her last years of illness, raised money for a monument at her gravesite. During her lifetime, Sojourner Truth was known more for the phrase, "Is God Dead?" than the phrase, "Ain't I a Woman?" This phrase, "Is God Dead?" was written on her gravestone.

Her friends and fellow activists mourned her and celebrated her memory. "Venerable for age, distinguished for insight into human nature, remarkable for independence and courageous self-assertion, devoted to the welfare of her race, she has been for the last forty years an object of respect and admiration to social reformers everywhere," wrote Frederick

Sojourner Truth and Abraham Lincoln

In 1893, Frances Titus commissioned an artist named Frank C. Courter to paint a portrait based on Truth's visit with Abraham Lincoln. The painting was the first of many images celebrating Sojourner Truth as a symbol of the equal rights cause. Over the years, she has appeared on posters, buttons, a United States postage stamp, and much more. However, this portrait is particularly interesting because of what Truth writes in her book, *Narrative of Sojourner Truth*. Truth went to see Lincoln with her friend, Lucy Coleman, a traveling companion who was white. Truth describes meeting Lincoln as a momentous occasion. During this meeting, he showed Truth the Bible that had been presented to him by African Americans in Baltimore. Truth is said to have felt she was in the presence of a friend and points out that the same hand who signed the Emancipation Proclamation signed the note to her in her "Book of Life." The portrait was unfortunately burned in a fire, but a photograph of the portrait lives on.

Douglass the day after her death. The women's rights activists Elizabeth Cady Stanton and Susan B. Anthony called Truth "the most wonderful woman the colored race has ever produced" in their *History of Woman Suffrage*. Frances Titus added "A Memorial Chapter" to *Narrative of Sojourner Truth* in 1884.

Dignity and Fire

The modern image of Sojourner Truth is largely a result of Frances Gage's account. Truth stands in our minds as a woman of color who bravely faced her opponents with dignity and fire. Her speech has become a similar type of legend as the story of George Washington chopping down the cherry tree and taking responsibility for his actions. Even if the events are more myth than fact, they still influence our view of George Washington and Sojourner Truth.

Without the dramatic background, Truth's "Ain't I a Woman?" speech still stands firmly as a landmark address. Truth straddled both the abolitionist and women's rights movements. By asking "Ain't I a woman?" she demanded acceptance as a black woman at a time when society considered blacks and women inferior. By referring to her life as a slave, she reminded the audience that was there solely to support women's rights of the evils of slavery.

Radical Views

Many women's rights activists advocated women's suffrage, legal rights, and expanded job opportunities. Truth did not address the practical issues of the women's rights movement at the Akron convention. Instead, she took

This portrait by Courter is called Lincoln Showing Sojourner Truth the Bible Presented Him by the Colored People of Baltimore.

a much more radical view, declaring that women were the physical and intellectual equals of men. Women of the nineteenth century were bound by strict social customs, and even many activists did not want to appear "unfeminine." Truth's conception of equality between men and women was not widely accepted until the twentieth century.

Today, Sojourner Truth stands as a symbol of someone who overcame hardship and worked for equal rights. She has been recognized by the National Women's Hall of Fame. Battle Creek, Michigan, has a Sojourner Truth Memorial Association and a Sojourner Truth Memorial Highway.

But Truth's legacy lies in her dedication to activism, not in awards and memorials. Truth lived to see slavery abolished, yet African Americans still faced discrimination. Women did not gain the right to vote during Truth's lifetime. Truth's work served as an inspiration for supporters of equal rights who followed in her footsteps. In 1920, the Nineteenth Amendment to the Constitution granted women the right to vote. Ninety years after Truth sued a Washington, DC, transit company, Rosa Parks's refusal to give up a bus seat inspired fresh support for the cause of equal rights. The civil rights movement of the 1950s and 1960s made great progress in the fight against racial discrimination. Today, activists for equality and social justice still carry on Sojourner Truth's work.

Truth's [illegible] states she was 105 [illegible]. She was actually 86 when she passed away.

PRIMARY SOURCE TRANSCRIPTIONS

Frances Gage's Version of Sojourner Truth's "Ain't I a Woman?" Speech

(Contemporary English Translation)

Well, children, where there is so much racket, there must be something out of kilter. I think that between the Negroes of the South and the women of the North, all talking about rights, the white men will be in a fix pretty soon. But what's all this here talking about?

That man over there says that women need to be helped into carriages, and lifted over ditches, and to have the best place everywhere. Nobody ever helps me into carriages, or over mud puddles, or gives me any best place! And ain't I a woman? Look at me! Look at my arm! I have plowed and planted, and gathered into barns, and no man could outdo me! And ain't I a woman? I could work as much and eat as much as a man—when I could get it—and bear the lash as well! And ain't I a woman? I have borne thirteen children and seen almost all of them sold off to slavery, and when I cried out with a mother's grief, none but Jesus heard me! And ain't I a woman?

Then they talk about this thing in the head; what's this they call it? (someone whispers, "Intellect"). That's it, honey. What's that have to do with women's rights or Negroes' rights? If my cup won't hold but a pint, and yours holds a quart, wouldn't you be mean not to let me have my little half measure full?

Then that little man in black there, he says women can't have as much rights as men, because Christ wasn't a woman! Where did your Christ come from? Where did your Christ come from? From God and a woman! Man had nothing to do with Him.

If the first woman God ever made was strong enough to turn the world upside down all alone, these women together ought to be able to turn it back, and get it right side up again! And now they are asking to do it, the men better let them.

I'm obliged to you for hearing me, and now old Sojourner ain't got nothing more to say.

Marius Robinson's Version of Sojourner Truth's "Ain't I a Woman?" Speech

I want to say a few words about this matter.

I am for woman's rights. I have as much muscle as any man, and can do as much work as any man. I have plowed and reaped and husked and chopped and mowed, and can any man do more than that? I have heard much about the sexes being equal. I can carry as much as any man, and can eat as much too, if I can get it. I am as strong as any man that is now.

As for intellect, all I can say is, if a woman have a pint, and a man a quart—why can't she have her little pint full? You need not be afraid to give us our rights for fear we will take too much—for we can't take more than our pint'll hold.

The poor men seems to be all in confusion, and don’t know what to do. Why children, if you have woman’s rights, give it to her and you will feel better. You will have your own rights, and they won’t be so much trouble.

I can’t read, but I can hear. I have heard the Bible and have learned that Eve caused man to sin. Well, if woman upset the world, do give her a chance to set it right side up again. The Lady has spoken about Jesus, how he never spurned woman from him, and she was right. When Lazarus died, Mary and Martha came to him with faith and love and besought him to raise their brother. And Jesus wept and Lazarus came forth. And how came Jesus into the world? Through God who created him and the woman who bore him. Man, where was your part?

But the women are coming up blessed be God and a few of the men are coming up with them. But man is in a tight place, the poor slave is on him, woman is coming on him, he is surely between a hawk and a buzzard.

CHRONOLOGY

ca. 1797 Sojourner Truth is born a slave named Isabella.

1810 Isabella is sold to the Dumont family.

1814 Isabella marries a slave named Thomas.

1815–1826 Isabella bears five children.

1826 Isabella leaves the Dumonts.

1827 Isabella sues to recover her son Peter, who had been sold into slavery in Alabama.

1829 Isabella moves to New York City.

1832 Isabella joins Matthias's Kingdom.

1843 Isabella leaves New York and renames herself Sojourner Truth.

1844 Truth settles in Northampton, Massachusetts.

1850 Truth publishes her *Narrative of Sojourner Truth*. Truth begins speaking out for the abolitionist cause and women's rights.

1851 Truth gives her "Ain't I a Woman?" address in Akron, Ohio.

1853 Truth visits Harriet Beecher Stowe.

1857 Truth moves to Michigan.

1863 Stowe publishes "Sojourner Truth, the Libyan Sibyl." Frances D. Gage publishes her account of the "Ain't I a Woman?" speech.

1864 Truth moves to Washington, DC, where she meets with President Lincoln and works on behalf of freedmen.

1865 Truth sues after being discriminated against and injured by a streetcar conductor.

1870 Truth begins calling for the resettlement of freedmen in the western territories.

1875 Truth publishes an updated version of her autobiography.

1879 Truth travels to Kansas to work with the Exodusters.

1883 Truth dies at her home in Battle Creek, Michigan.

GLOSSARY

abolition Ending slavery.

Amazon In Greek mythology, a member of a nation of female warriors.

charismatic Having the ability to attract others easily, often through personality.

contentious Causing or likely to cause conflict.

cooperative An enterprise or organization owned and managed jointly by those who make use of its facilities or services.

cult Usually any small religious group outside the mainstream and often dismissed as fraudulent.

delegate A representative.

dialect A variety of language specific to a certain region, culture, or place.

emancipation The act of freeing from the restraint, control, or power of another, usually referring to the freeing of slaves.

endorse To openly approve of.

feminist One who believes in or works for women's political, economic, and social equality with men.

fervor Intense enthusiasm.

Homestead Act An act passed by Congress in 1862 promising ownership of a 160-acre (65-hectare) tract of public land to a citizen or head of a family who had lived on and farmed the land for five years after the initial claim.

Quaker A member of the Christian group the Religious Society of Friends, which preaches kindness and nonviolence.

Reconstruction The period (1865–1877) during which the states that had seceded were controlled by the federal government before being readmitted to the Union.

secede To formally withdraw from an organization.

sibyl Fortune teller.

spiritualism A philosophical and religious movement that believes in the possibility of communicating with souls after death.

Universalists A religious group believing in the eventual salvation of all of humanity.

BIBLIOGRAPHY

Coates, Steve. "Abraham Lincoln and Sojourner Truth." *New York Times*, October 29, 2010. https://artsbeat.blogs.nytimes.com/2010/10/29/abraham-lincoln-and-sojourner-truth/.

"Compare the Speeches." The Sojourner Truth Project. Retrieved April 10, 2019. https://www.thesojournertruthproject.com/compare-the-speeches/.

Delagarza, Kristina. "A Riot for Rights: Gabriel Prosser's Slave Revolt." Not Even Past, August 22, 2014. https://notevenpast.org/a-riot-for-rights-gabriel-prossers-slave-revolt/.

Dudley, William, ed. *American Slavery*. San Diego, CA: Greenhaven Press, 2000.

"Her History." Sojourner Truth Memorial Committee. November 16, 2017. https://sojournertruthmemorial.org/sojourner-truth/her-history/.

Mabee, Carleton, with Susan Mabee Newhouse. *Sojourner Truth—Slave, Prophet, Legend*. New York, NY: New York University Press, 1995.

Mandziuk, Roseann M. "'Grotesque and Ludicrous, but Yet Inspiring': Depictions of Sojourner Truth and Rhetorics of Domination." *Quarterly Journal of Speech* 100, no. 4 (2014): 467–87.

Painter, Nell Irvin, ed. *Narrative of Sojourner Truth*. New York, NY: Penguin Books, 1998.

Painter, Nell Irvin. *Sojourner Truth, a Life, a Symbol*. New York, NY: W. W. Norton and Company, 1996.

Stalcup, Brenda, ed. *Women's Suffrage*. San Diego, CA: Greenhaven Press, 2000.

Stetson, Erlene, and Linda David. *Glorying in Tribulation: The Lifework of Sojourner Truth*. East Lansing, MI: Michigan State University Press, 1994.

Washington, Margaret. *Sojourner Truth's America*. Urbana, IL: University of Illinois Press, 2011.

FURTHER READING

Books

Randolph, Joanne. *Abolitionists Join the Fight*. New York, NY: PowerKids Press, 2018.

Robinson, Natasha Sistrunk. *A Sojourner's Truth: Choosing Freedom and Courage in a Divided World*. Downers Grove, IL: InterVarsity Press, 2018.

Truth, Sojourner. *The Narrative of Sojourner Truth*. Los Angeles, CA: Enhanced Media Publishing, 2017.

Walker, David F., James Guy Hill, Marissa Louise, and Damon Smith. *The Life of Frederick Douglass: A Graphic Narrative of a Slave's Journey from Bondage to Freedom*. New York, NY: Ten Speed Press, 2018.

Websites

Library of Congress

www.loc.gov/item/today-in-history/november-26/

The Library of Congress documents aspects of Sojourner Truth's life, especially when she and Abraham Lincoln met.

Sojourner Truth

www.womenshistory.org/education-resources/biographies/sojourner-truth

This page offers a brief history of Sojourner Truth's life.

The Underground Railroad

www.pbs.org/wgbh/aia/part4/4p2944.html

Learn about the history of the Underground Railroad.

INDEX